THE BANJO'S BEST-LOVED POEMS

THE BANJO'S
best-loved poems

CHOSEN BY HIS GRAND~DAUGHTERS
ILLUSTRATED BY OUTBACK ARTIST HUGH SAWREY

NEW
HOLLAND

Foreword

The selection of "family favourites" for an illustrated volume of our grandfather's poetry is a task which has given us a great deal of pleasure. Of the poems we have included, some would rank as overall favourites while others have a special appeal to one or another member of the family. Many of the poems have been familiar to us since our earliest childhood. Even before we could read, our mother recited poetry of all kinds to us.

Two of the poems in this collection, namely "A Grain of Desert Sand" and "The Uplift", will be new to many readers, as they first appeared in print with the publication of our grandfather's Complete Literary Works in 1983. Mother was always particularly fond of "A Grain of Desert Sand" and it is through her excellent memory that we have been able to include it. It was sent home to his children with a letter when grandfather served with the Remount Forces in Egypt during the First World War.

We are quite often asked "What is your favourite poem?" and "Are you able to recite every word your grandfather wrote?" As to the latter, the answer is No; as to the former, it would be hard to single out one poem in particular. However, our tastes have changed very little over the years and childhood favourites are still favourites today. Poems such as "The Man from Snowy River" appealed to us for their rhythm and excitement and continue to do so. While the fact that the poetry was written by our grandfather was not stressed at home, one of us does remember, as a very young child, Mother making a point of explaining that "The Man from Snowy River" had been written by him. (Incidentally, it was a puzzle for years why the stockmen had "mustard" at the homestead overnight!)

Saltbush Bill and his various exploits played a very large part in our lives and we include the first two poems in this series. We have also included a selection of our favourite racing poems, such as "The Amateur Rider" and "The Old Timer's Steeplechase".

The Paterson brand of humour is shared by all the family and explains our particular fondness for many of the poems in this selection. "Any Other Time", "Those Names", and "A Bush Christening" are included for this reason. "The Geebung Polo Club" has a special place in our memory. The illustrations by Frank Mahony, which appeared with the poem when it was originally published, always hung in the hallway at home and added point to the humour.

Of course, it wasn't only the humorous and exciting poems that appealed to us. No collection of family favourites would be complete without "Clancy of The Overflow", "Black Swans", and "By the Grey Gulf-water", which are in a category of their own and bring home to us our grandfather's great love of the bush.

Many of the verses, when published originally in magazines such as the *Bulletin* and the *Sydney Mail*, were illustrated by contemporary artists and we have always felt that his poetry lends itself well to illustration. We are delighted with this new and exciting artwork by Hugh Sawrey. He has, indeed, captured the spirit of the poems and the moods and colours of the bush and its characters. We hope the book will give you as much pleasure as it gives us.

Rosamund Campbell and Philippa Harvie
Sydney, 1985

Contents

A Singer of the Bush

There is waving of grass in the breeze
   And a song in the air,
And a murmur of myriad bees
   That toil everywhere.
There is scent in the blossom and bough,
   And the breath of the spring
Is as soft as a kiss on a brow —
   And springtime I sing.

There is drought on the land, and the stock
   Tumble down in their tracks
Or follow — a tottering flock —
   The scrub-cutter's axe.
While ever a creature survives
   The axes shall swing;
We are fighting with fate for their lives —
   And the combat I sing.

The Man from Snowy River

There was movement at the station, for the word had passed around
    That the colt from old Regret had got away,
And had joined the wild bush horses — he was worth a thousand pound,
    So all the cracks had gathered to the fray.
All the tried and noted riders from the stations near and far
    Had mustered at the homestead overnight,
For the bushmen love hard riding where the wild bush horses are,
    And the stockhorse snuffs the battle with delight.

There was Harrison, who made his pile when Pardon won the cup,
    The old man with his hair as white as snow;
But few could ride beside him when his blood was fairly up —
    He would go wherever horse and man could go.
And Clancy of the Overflow came down to lend a hand,
    No better horseman ever held the reins;
For never horse could throw him while the saddle girths would stand,
    He learnt to ride while droving on the plains.

And one was there, a stripling on a small and weedy beast,
    He was something like a racehorse undersized,
With a touch of Timor pony — three parts thoroughbred at least —
    And such as are by mountain horsemen prized.
He was hard and tough and wiry — just the sort that won't say die —
    There was courage in his quick impatient tread;
And he bore the badge of gameness in his bright and fiery eye,
    And the proud and lofty carriage of his head.

But still so slight and weedy, one would doubt his power to stay,
    And the old man said, "That horse will never do
For a long and tiring gallop — lad, you'd better stop away,
    Those hills are far too rough for such as you."
So he waited sad and wistful — only Clancy stood his friend —

"I think we ought to let him come," he said;
"I warrant he'll be with us when he's wanted at the end,
  For both his horse and he are mountain bred.

"He hails from Snowy River, up by Kosciusko's side,
  Where the hills are twice as steep and twice as rough,
Where a horse's hoofs strike firelight from the flint stones every stride,
  The man that holds his own is good enough.
And the Snowy River riders on the mountains make their home,
  Where the river runs those giant hills between;
I have seen full many horsemen since I first commenced to roam,
  But nowhere yet such horsemen have I seen."

So he went — they found the horses by the big mimosa clump —
  They raced away towards the mountain's brow,
And the old man gave his orders, "Boys, go at them from the jump,
  No use to try for fancy riding now.
And, Clancy, you must wheel them, try and wheel them to the right.
  Ride boldly, lad, and never fear the spills,
For never yet was rider that could keep the mob in sight,
  If once they gain the shelter of those hills."

So Clancy rode to wheel them — he was racing on the wing
  Where the best and boldest riders take their place,
And he raced his stockhorse past them, and he made the ranges ring
  With the stockwhip, as he met them face to face.
Then they halted for a moment, while he swung the dreaded lash,
  But they saw their well-loved mountain full in view,
And they charged beneath the stockwhip with a sharp and sudden dash,
  And off into the mountain scrub they flew.

Then fast the horsemen followed, where the gorges deep and black
  Resounded to the thunder of their tread,
And the stockwhips woke the echoes, and they fiercely answered back
  From cliffs and crags that beetled overhead.

And upward, ever upward, the wild horses held their way,
    Where mountain ash and kurrajong grew wide;
And the old man muttered fiercely, "We may bid the mob good day,
    No man can hold them down the other side."

When they reached the mountain's summit, even Clancy took a pull,
    It well might make the boldest hold their breath,
The wild hop scrub grew thickly, and the hidden ground was full
    Of wombat holes, and any slip was death.
But the man from Snowy River let the pony have his head,
    And he swung his stockwhip round and gave a cheer,
And he raced him down the mountain like a torrent down its bed,
    While the others stood and watched in very fear.

He sent the flint stones flying, but the pony kept his feet,
    He cleared the fallen timber in his stride,
And the man from Snowy River never shifted in his seat —
    It was grand to see that mountain horseman ride.
Through the stringybarks and saplings, on the rough and broken ground,
    Down the hillside at a racing pace he went;
And he never drew the bridle till he landed safe and sound,
    At the bottom of that terrible descent.

He was right among the horses as they climbed the further hill,
    And the watchers on the mountain standing mute,
Saw him ply the stockwhip fiercely, he was right among them still,
    As he raced across the clearing in pursuit.
Then they lost him for a moment, where two mountain gullies met
    In the ranges, but a final glimpse reveals
On a dim and distant hillside the wild horses racing yet,
    With the man from Snowy River at their heels.

And he ran them single-handed till their sides were white with foam.
    He followed like a bloodhound on their track,
Till they halted cowed and beaten, then he turned their heads for home,
    And alone and unassisted brought them back.
But his hardy mountain pony he could scarcely raise a trot,
    He was blood from hip to shoulder from the spur;
But his pluck was still undaunted, and his courage fiery hot,
    For never yet was mountain horse a cur.

And down by Kosciusko, where the pine-clad ridges raise
    Their torn and rugged battlements on high,
Where the air is clear as crystal, and the white stars fairly blaze
    At midnight in the cold and frosty sky,
And where around The Overflow the reed beds sweep and sway
    To the breezes, and the rolling plains are wide,
The man from Snowy River is a household word today,
    And the stockmen tell the story of his ride.

Pioneers

They came of bold and roving stock that would not fixed abide;
   They were the sons of field and flock since e'er they learned to ride;
We may not hope to see such men in these degenerate years
As those explorers of the bush — the brave old pioneers.

'Twas they who rode the trackless bush in heat and storm and drought;
'Twas they that heard the master-word that called them further out;
'Twas they that followed up the trail the mountain cattle made
And pressed across the mighty range where now their bones are laid.

But now the times are dull and slow, the brave old days are dead
When hardy bushmen started out, and forced their way ahead
By tangled scrub and forests grim towards the unknown west,
And spied the far-off promised land from off the ranges' crest.

Oh! ye, that sleep in lonely graves by far-off ridge and plain,
We drink to you in silence now as Christmas comes again,
The men who fought the wilderness through rough, unsettled years —
The founders of our nation's life, the brave old pioneers.

The Man from Ironbark

It was the man from Ironbark who struck the Sydney town,
He wandered over street and park, he wandered up and down.
He loitered here, he loitered there, till he was like to drop,
Until at last in sheer despair he sought a barber's shop.
"'Ere! shave my beard and whiskers off, I'll be a man of mark,
I'll go and do the Sydney toff up home in Ironbark."

The barber man was small and flash, as barbers mostly are,
He wore a strike-your-fancy sash, he smoked a huge cigar;
He was a humorist of note and keen at repartee,
He laid the odds and kept a "tote", whatever that may be,
And when he saw our friend arrive, he whispered, "Here's a lark!
Just watch me catch him all alive, this man from Ironbark."

There were some gilded youths that sat along the barber's wall.
Their eyes were dull, their heads were flat, they had no brains at all;
To them the barber passed the wink, his dexter eyelid shut,
"I'll make this bloomin' yokel think his bloomin' throat is cut."
And as he soaped and rubbed it in he made a rude remark:
"I s'pose the flats is pretty green up there in Ironbark."

A grunt was all reply he got; he shaved the bushman's chin,
Then made the water boiling hot and dipped the razor in.
He raised his hand, his brow grew black, he paused awhile to gloat,
Then slashed the red-hot razor back across his victim's throat;
Upon the newly-shaven skin it made a livid mark —
No doubt it fairly took him in — the man from Ironbark.

He fetched a wild up-country yell might wake the dead to hear,
And though his throat, he knew full well, was cut from ear to ear,
He struggled gamely to his feet, and faced the murd'rous foe:
"You've done for me! you dog, I'm beat! one hit before I go!

I only wish I had a knife, you blessed murdering shark!
But you'll remember all your life the man from Ironbark."

He lifted up his hairy paw, with one tremendous clout
He landed on the barber's jaw, and knocked the barber out.
He set to work with nail and tooth, he made the place a wreck;
He grabbed the nearest gilded youth, and tried to break his neck.
And all the while his throat he held to save his vital spark,
And "Murder! Bloody murder!" yelled the man from Ironbark.

A peeler who had heard the din came in to see the show;
He tried to run the bushman in, but he refused to go.
And when at last the barber spoke, and said "'Twas all in fun —
'Twas just a little harmless joke, a trifle overdone."
"A joke!" he cried, "By George, that's fine; a lively sort of lark;
I'd like to catch that murdering swine some night in Ironbark."

And now while round the shearing floor the list'ning shearers gape,
He tells the story o'er and o'er, and brags of his escape.
"Them barber chaps what keeps a tote, By George, I've had enough,
One tried to cut my bloomin' throat, but thank the Lord it's tough."
And whether he's believed or no, there's one thing to remark,
That flowing beards are all the go way up in Ironbark.

Clancy of The Overflow

I had written him a letter which I had, for want of better
   Knowledge, sent to where I met him down the Lachlan, years ago,
He was shearing when I knew him, so I sent the letter to him,
   Just "on spec", addressed as follows: "Clancy, of The Overflow".

And an answer came directed in a writing unexpected,
   (And I think the same was written with a thumbnail dipped in tar)
'Twas his shearing mate who wrote it, and *verbatim* I will quote it:
   "Clancy's gone to Queensland droving, and we don't know where
      he are."

In my wild erratic fancy visions come to me of Clancy
   Gone a-droving "down the Cooper" where the western drovers go;
As the stock are slowly stringing, Clancy rides behind them singing,
   For the drover's life has pleasures that the townsfolk never know.

And the bush hath friends to meet him, and their kindly voices greet him
   In the murmur of the breezes and the river on its bars,
And he sees the vision splendid of the sunlit plains extended,
   And at night the wondrous glory of the everlasting stars.

I am sitting in my dingy little office, where a stingy
   Ray of sunlight struggles feebly down between the houses tall,
And the foetid air and gritty of the dusty, dirty city
   Through the open window floating, spreads its foulness over all.

And in place of lowing cattle, I can hear the fiendish rattle
   Of the tramways and the buses making hurry down the street,
And the language uninviting of the gutter children fighting,
   Comes fitfully and faintly through the ceaseless tramp of feet.

And the hurrying people daunt me, and their pallid faces haunt me
   As they shoulder one another in their rush and nervous haste,
With their eager eyes and greedy, and their stunted forms and weedy,
   For townsfolk have no time to grow, they have no time to waste.

And I somehow rather fancy that I'd like to change with Clancy,
   Like to take a turn at droving where the seasons come and go,
While he faced the round eternal of the cashbook and the journal —
   But I doubt he'd suit the office, Clancy, of "The Overflow".

On Kiley's Run

The roving breezes come and go
   On Kiley's Run,
The sleepy river murmurs low,
And far away one dimly sees
Beyond the stretch of forest trees —
Beyond the foothills dusk and dun —
The ranges sleeping in the sun
   On Kiley's Run.

'Tis many years since first I came
   To Kiley's Run,
More years than I would care to name
Since I, a stripling, used to ride
For miles and miles at Kiley's side,
The while in stirring tones he told
The stories of the days of old
   On Kiley's Run.

I see the old bush homestead now
   On Kiley's Run,
Just nestled down beneath the brow
Of one small ridge above the sweep
Of river flat, where willows weep
And jasmine flowers and roses bloom,
The air was laden with perfume
   On Kiley's Run.

We lived the good old station life
   On Kiley's Run,
With little thought of care or strife.
Old Kiley seldom used to roam,
He liked to make the Run his home,

The swagman never turned away
With empty hand at close of day
   From Kiley's Run.

We kept a racehorse now and then
   On Kiley's Run,
And neighb'ring stations brought their men
To meetings where the sport was free,
And dainty ladies came to see
Their champions ride; with laugh and song
The old house rang the whole night long
   On Kiley's Run.

The station hands were friends I wot
   On Kiley's Run,
A reckless, merry-hearted lot —
All splendid riders, and they knew
The "boss" was kindness through and through.
Old Kiley always stood their friend,
And so they served him to the end
   On Kiley's Run.

But droughts and losses came apace
   To Kiley's Run,
Till ruin stared him in the face;
He toiled and toiled while lived the light,
He dreamed of overdrafts at night:
At length, because he could not pay,
His bankers took the stock away
   From Kiley's Run.

Old Kiley stood and saw them go
   From Kiley's Run.
The well-bred cattle marching slow;
His stockmen, mates for many a day,
They wrung his hand and went away.

26

Too old to make another start,
Old Kiley died — of broken heart,
  On Kiley's Run.

The owner lives in England now
  Of Kiley's Run.
He knows a racehorse from a cow;
But that is all he knows of stock:
His chiefest care is how to dock
Expenses, and he sends from town
To cut the shearers' wages down
  On Kiley's Run.

There are no neighbours anywhere
  Near Kiley's Run.
The hospitable homes are bare,
The gardens gone; for no pretence
Must hinder cutting down expense:
The homestead that we held so dear
Contains a half-paid overseer
  On Kiley's Run.

The life and sport and hope have died
    On Kiley's Run.
No longer there the stockmen ride;
For sour-faced boundary riders creep
On mongrel horses after sheep,
Through ranges where, at racing speed,
Old Kiley used to "wheel the lead"
    On Kiley's Run.

There runs a lane for thirty miles
    Through Kiley's Run.
On either side the herbage smiles,
But wretched trav'lling sheep must pass
Without a drink or blade of grass
Thro' that long lane of death and shame:
The weary drovers curse the name
    Of Kiley's Run.

The name itself is changed of late
    Of Kiley's Run.
They call it "Chandos Park Estate".
The lonely swagman through the dark
Must hump his swag past Chandos Park.
The name is English, don't you see,
The old name sweeter sounds to me
    Of "Kiley's Run".

I cannot guess what fate will bring
    To Kiley's Run —
For chances come and changes ring —
I scarcely think 'twill always be
Locked up to suit an absentee;
And if he lets it out in farms
His tenants soon will carry arms
    On Kiley's Run.

The Old Timer's Steeplechase

The sheep were shorn and the wool went down
   At the time of our local racing:
And I'd earned a spell — I was burnt and brown —
So I rolled my swag for a trip to town
   And a look at the steeplechasing.

'Twas rough and ready — an uncleared course
   As rough as the blacks had found it;
With barbed wire fences, topped with gorse,
And a water jump that would drown a horse,
   And the steeple three times round it.

There was never a fence the tracks to guard —
   Some straggling posts defined 'em:
And the day was hot, and the drinking hard,
Till none of the stewards could see a yard
   Before nor yet behind 'em!

But the bell was rung and the nags were out,
   Excepting an old outsider
Whose trainer started an awful rout,
For his boy had gone on a drinking bout
   And left him without a rider.

"Is there not one man in the crowd," he cried,
   "In the whole of the crowd so clever,
Is there not one man that will take a ride
On the old white horse from the northern side
   That was bred on the Mooki River?"

'Twas an old white horse that they called The Cow,
    And a cow would look well beside him;
But I was pluckier then than now
(And I wanted excitement anyhow),
    So at last I agreed to ride him.

And the trainer said, "Well, he's dreadful slow,
    And he hasn't a chance whatever;
But I'm stony broke, so it's time to show
A trick or two that the trainers know
    Who train by the Mooki River.

"The first time round at the further side,
    With the trees and the scrub about you,
Just pull behind them and run out wide
And then dodge into the scrub and hide,
    And let them go round without you.

"At the third time round, for the final spin
  With the pace, and the dust to blind 'em,
They'll never notice if you chip in
For the last half-mile — you'll be sure to win,
  And they'll think you raced behind 'em.

"At the water jump you may have to swim —
  He hasn't a hope to clear it —
Unless he skims like the swallows skim
At full speed over, but not for him!
  He'll never go next or near it.

"But don't you worry — just plunge across,
  For he swims like a well-trained setter.
Then hide away in the scrub and gorse
The rest will be far ahead of course —
  The further ahead the better.

"You must rush the jumps in the last half-round
　　For fear that he might refuse 'em;
He'll try to baulk with you, I'll be bound,
Take whip and spurs on the mean old hound,
　　And don't be afraid to use 'em.

"At the final round, when the field are slow
　　And you are quite fresh to meet 'em,
Sit down, and hustle him all you know
With the whip and spurs, and he'll have to go —
　　Remember, you've *got* to beat 'em!"

The flag went down and we seemed to fly,
　　And we made the timbers shiver
Of the first big fence, as the stand flashed by,
And I caught the ring of the trainer's cry:
　　"Go on! For the Mooki River!"

I jammed him in with a well-packed crush,
　　And recklessly — out for slaughter —
Like a living wave over fence and brush
We swept and swung with a flying rush,
　　Till we came to the dreaded water.

Ha, ha! I laugh at it now to think
　　Of the way I contrived to work it.
Shut in amongst them, before you'd wink,
He found himself on the water's brink,
　　With never a chance to shirk it!

The thought of the horror he felt, beguiles
　　The heart of this grizzled rover!
He gave a snort you could hear for miles,
And a spring would have cleared the Channel Isles
　　And carried me safely over!

Then we neared the scrub, and I pulled him back
  In the shade where the gum leaves quiver:
And I waited there in the shadows black
While the rest of the horses, round the track,
  Went on like a rushing river!

At the second round, as the field swept by,
  I saw that the pace was telling;
But on they thundered, and by and by
As they passed the stand I could hear the cry
  Of the folk in the distance, yelling!

Then the last time round! And the hoofbeats rang!
   And I said, "Well, it's now or never!"
And out on the heels of the throng I sprang,
And the spurs bit deep and the whipcord sang
   As I rode! For the Mooki River!

We raced for home in a cloud of dust
   And the curses rose in chorus.
'Twas flog, and hustle, and jump you must!
And The Cow ran well — but to my disgust
   There was one got home before us.

'Twas a big black horse, that I had not seen
   In the part of the race I'd ridden;
And his coat was cool and his rider clean,
And I thought that perhaps I had not been
   The only one that had hidden.

And the trainer came with a visage blue
   With rage, when the race concluded:
Said he, "I thought you'd have pulled us through,
But the man on the black horse planted too,
   And nearer to home than you did!"

Alas to think that those times so gay
   Have vanished and passed forever!
You don't believe in the yarn you say?
Why, man! 'Twas a matter of every day
   When we raced on the Mooki River!

Shearing at Castlereagh

The bell is set a-ringing, and the engine gives a toot,
  There's five and thirty shearers here a-shearing for the loot,
So stir yourselves, you penners-up and shove the sheep along,
The musterers are fetching them a hundred thousand strong,
And make your collie dogs speak up — what would the buyers say
In London if the wool was late this year from Castlereagh?

The man that "rung" the Tubbo shed is not the ringer here,
That stripling from the Cooma side can teach him how to shear.
They trim away the ragged locks, and rip the cutter goes,
And leaves a track of snowy fleece from brisket to the nose;
It's lovely how they peel it off with never stop nor stay,
They're racing for the ringer's place this year at Castlereagh.

The man that keeps the cutters sharp is growling in his cage,
He's always in a hurry and he's always in a rage —
"You clumsy-fisted muttonheads, you'd turn a fellow sick,
You pass yourselves as shearers? You were born to swing a pick!
Another broken cutter here, that's two you've broke today,
It's awful how such crawlers come to shear at Castlereagh."

The youngsters picking up the fleece enjoy the merry din,
They throw the classer up the fleece, he throws it to the bin;
The pressers standing by the rack are waiting for the wool,
There's room for just a couple more, the press is nearly full;
Now jump upon the lever, lads, and heave and heave away,
Another bale of golden fleece is branded "Castlereagh".

Any Other Time

All of us play our very best game —
    Any other time.
Golf or billiards, it's all the same —
    Any other time.
Lose a match and you always say,
"Just my luck! I was 'off' to-day!
I could have beaten him quite halfway —
    Any other time!"

After a fiver you ought to go —
    Any other time.
Every man that you ask says "Oh,
    Any *other* time.
Lend you a fiver! I'd lend you two,
But I'm overdrawn and my bills are due,
Wish you'd ask me — now, mind you do —
    Any other time!"

Fellows will ask you out to dine —
    Any other time.
"Not tonight, for we're twenty-nine —
    Any other time.
Not tomorrow, for cook's on strike —
Not next day, I'll be out on the bike —
Just drop in whenever you like —
    Any other time!"

Seasick passengers like the sea —
    Any other time.
"Something . . . I ate . . . disagreed . . . with me!
    Any other time
Ocean-trav'lling is . . . simply bliss,

Must be my . . . liver . . . has gone amiss . . .
Why, I would laugh . . . at a sea . . . like this —
    Any other time."

Most of us mean to be better men —
    Any other time:
Regular upright characters then —
    Any other time.
Yet somehow as the years go by
Still we gamble and drink and lie,
When it comes to the last we'll want to die —
    Any other time!

Saltbush Bill

Now this is the law of the Overland that all in the west obey,
A man must cover with travelling sheep a six-mile stage a day;
But this is the law which the drovers make, right easily understood,
They travel their stage where the grass is bad, but they camp where the
    grass is good;
They camp, and they ravage the squatter's grass till never a
    blade remains,
Then they drift away as the white clouds drift on the edge of the
    saltbush plains,
From camp to camp and from run to run they battle it hand to hand,
For a blade of grass and the right to pass on the track of the Overland.

For this is the law of the Great Stock Routes, 'tis written in white
    and black —
The man that goes with a travelling mob must keep to a half-mile track;
And the drovers keep to a half-mile track on the runs where the grass
    is dead,
But they spread their sheep on a well-grassed run till they go with a
    two-mile spread.
So the squatters hurry the drovers on from dawn till the fall of night,
And the squatters' dogs and the drovers' dogs get mixed in a deadly fight;
Yet the squatters' men though they hunt the mob, are willing the peace
    to keep,
For the drovers learn how to use their hands when they go with the
    travelling sheep;
But this is the tale of a Jackaroo that came from a foreign strand,
And the fight that he fought with Saltbush Bill, the King of the Overland.

Now Saltbush Bill was a drover tough, as ever the country knew,
He had fought his way on the Great Stock Routes from the sea to the
    Big Barcoo;

He could tell when he came to a friendly run that gave him a chance
    to spread,
And he knew where the hungry owners were that hurried his
    sheep ahead;
He was drifting down in the Eighty drought with a mob that could
    scarcely creep,
(When the kangaroos by the thousands starve, it is rough on the
    travelling sheep.)
And he camped one night at the crossing place on the edge of the
    Wilga run,
"We must manage a feed for them here," he said, "or the half of the mob
    are done!"
So he spread them out when they left the camp wherever they liked to go,
Till he grew aware of a Jackaroo with a station hand in tow,

And they set to work on the straggling sheep, and with many
     a stockwhip crack
They forced them in where the grass was dead in the space of the
     half-mile track;
So William prayed that the hand of fate might suddenly strike him blue
But he'd get some grass for his starving sheep in the teeth of that
     Jackaroo.
So he turned and he cursed the Jackaroo, he cursed him alive or dead,
From the soles of his great unwieldy feet to the crown of his ugly head,
With an extra curse on the moke he rode and the cur at his heels
     that ran,
Till the Jackaroo from his horse got down and he went for the
     drover man;
With the station hand for his picker-up, though the sheep ran loose
     the while,
They battled it out on the saltbush plain in the regular prize ring style.

Now, the new chum fought for his honour's sake and the pride of the
     English race,
But the drover fought for his daily bread with a smile on his bearded face;
So he shifted ground and he sparred for wind and he made it a
     lengthy mill,
And from time to time as his scouts came in they whispered to
     Saltbush Bill —
"We have spread the sheep with a two-mile spread, and the grass it is
     something grand,
You must stick to him, Bill, for another round for the pride of the
     Overland."

The new chum made it a rushing fight, though never a blow got home,
Till the sun rode high in the cloudless sky and glared on the
     brick-red loam,
Till the sheep drew in to the shelter trees and settled them down to rest,
Then the drover said he would fight no more and he gave his
     opponent best.

So the new chum rode to the homestead straight and he told them a
    story grand
Of the desperate fight that he fought that day with the King of
    the Overland.
And the tale went home to the public schools of the pluck of the
    English swell,
How the drover fought for his very life, but blood in the end must tell.
But the travelling sheep and the Wilga sheep were boxed on the Old
    Man Plain.
'Twas a full week's work ere they drafted out and hunted them off again,
With a week's good grass in their wretched hides, with a curse and a
    stockwhip crack,
They hunted them off on the road once more to starve on the
    half-mile track.
And Saltbush Bill, on the Overland, will many a time recite
How the best day's work that ever he did was the day that he lost
    the fight.

SAWKEY

Song of the Wheat

We have sung the song of the droving days,
  Of the march of the travelling sheep;
By silent stages and lonely ways
  Thin, white battalions creep.
But the man who now by the land would thrive
  Must his spurs to a ploughshare beat.
Is there ever a man in the world alive
  To sing the song of the Wheat!

It's west by south of the Great Divide
  The grim grey plains run out,
Where the old flock masters lived and died
  In a ceaseless fight with drought.
Weary with waiting and hope deferred
  They were ready to own defeat,
Till at last they heard the master-word
  And the master-word was Wheat.

Yarran and Myall and Box and Pine —
  'Twas axe and fire for all;
They scarce could tarry to blaze the line
  Or wait for the trees to fall,
Ere the team was yoked and the gates flung wide,
  And the dust of the horses' feet
Rose up like a pillar of smoke to guide
  The wonderful march of Wheat.

Furrow by furrow, and fold by fold,
  The soil is turned on the plain;
Better than silver and better than gold
  Is the surface-mine of the grain.
Better than cattle and better than sheep

In the fight with the drought and heat.
For a streak of stubbornness wide and deep
    Lies hid in a grain of Wheat.

When the stock is swept by the hand of fate,
    Deep down in his bed of clay
The brave brown Wheat will lie and wait
    For the resurrection day:
Lie hid while the whole world thinks him dead;
    But the spring rain, soft and sweet,
Will over the steaming paddocks spread
    The first green flush of the Wheat.

Green and amber and gold it grows
  When the sun sinks late in the west
And the breeze sweeps over the rippling rows
  Where the quail and the skylark nest.
Mountain or river or shining star,
  There's never a sight can beat —
Away to the skyline stretching far —
  A sea of the ripening Wheat.

When the burning harvest sun sinks low,
  And the shadows stretch on the plain,
The roaring strippers come and go
  Like ships on a sea of grain;
Till the lurching, groaning waggons bear
  Their tale of the load complete.
Of the world's great work he has done his share
  Who has gathered a crop of Wheat.

Princes and Potentates and Czars,
  They travel in regal state,
But old King Wheat has a thousand cars
  For his trip to the water-gate;
And his thousand steamships breast the tide
  And plough thro' the wind and sleet
To the lands where the teeming millions bide
  That say, "Thank God for Wheat!"

As Long as Your Eyes are Blue

Wilt thou love me, sweet, when my hair is grey,
   And my cheeks shall have lost their hue?
When the charms of youth shall have passed away,
   Will your love as of old prove true?
For the looks may change, and the heart may range,
   And the love be no longer fond;
Wilt thou love with truth in the years of youth
   And away to the years beyond?

Oh, I love you, sweet, for your locks of brown
   And the blush on your cheek that lies —
But I love you most for the kindly heart
   That I see in your sweet blue eyes —
For the eyes are signs of the soul within,
   Of the heart that is leal and true,
And mine own sweetheart, I shall love you still,
   Just as long as your eyes are blue.

For the locks may bleach, and the cheeks of peach
   May be reft of their golden hue;
But mine own sweetheart, I shall love you still,
   Just as long as your eyes are blue.

Father Riley's Horse

'T was the horse thief, Andy Regan, that was hunted like a dog
    By the troopers of the upper Murray side,
They had searched in every gully — they had looked in every log,
    But never sight or track of him they spied,
Till the priest at Kiley's Crossing heard a knocking very late
    And a whisper "Father Riley — come across!"
So his Rev'rence in pyjamas trotted softly to the gate
    And admitted Andy Regan — and a horse!

"Now, it's listen, Father Riley, to the words I've got to say,
    For it's close upon my death I am tonight.
With the troopers hard behind me I've been hiding all the day
    In the gullies keeping close and out of sight.
But they're watching all the ranges till there's not a bird could fly,
    And I'm fairly worn to pieces with the strife,
So I'm taking no more trouble, but I'm going home to die,
    'Tis the only way I see to save my life.

"Yes, I'm making home to mother's, and I'll die o' Tuesday next
    An' be buried on the Thursday — and, of course,
I'm prepared to meet my penance, but with one thing I'm perplexed
    And it's — Father, it's this jewel of a horse!
He was never bought nor paid for, and there's not a man can swear
    To his owner or his breeder, but I know,
That his sire was by Pedantic from the Old Pretender mare
    And his dam was close related to The Roe.

"And there's nothing in the district that can race him for a step,
    He could canter while they're going at their top:
He's the king of all the leppers that was ever seen to lep,
    A five-foot fence — he'd clear it in a hop!

So I'll leave him with you, Father, till the dead shall rise again,
    'Tis yourself that knows a good 'un; and, of course,
You can say he's got by Moonlight out of Paddy Murphy's plain
    If you're ever asked the breeding of the horse!

"But it's getting on to daylight and it's time to say goodbye,
    For the stars above the east are growing pale.
And I'm making home to mother — and it's hard for me to die!
    But it's harder still, is keeping out of gaol!
You can ride the old horse over to my grave across the dip
    Where the wattle bloom is waving overhead.
Sure he'll jump them fences easy — you must never raise the whip
    Or he'll rush 'em! — now, goodbye!" and he had fled!

So they buried Andy Regan, and they buried him to rights,
    In the graveyard at the back of Kiley's Hill;
There were five-and-twenty mourners who had five-and-twenty fights
    Till the very boldest fighters had their fill.
There were fifty horses racing from the graveyard to the pub,
    And their riders flogged each other all the while.
And the lashin's of the liquor! And the lavin's of the grub!
    Oh, poor Andy went to rest in proper style.

Then the races came to Kiley's — with a steeplechase and all,
    For the folk were mostly Irish round about,
And it takes an Irish rider to be fearless of a fall,
    They were training morning in and morning out.
But they never started training till the sun was on the course,
    For a superstitious story kept 'em back,
That the ghost of Andy Regan on a slashing chestnut horse,
    Had been training by the starlight on the track.

And they read the nominations for the races with surprise
    And amusement at the Father's little joke,
For a novice had been entered for the steeplechasing prize,
    And they found that it was Father Riley's moke!

He was neat enough to gallop, he was strong enough to stay!
    But his owner's views of training were immense,
For the Reverend Father Riley used to ride him every day,
    And he never saw a hurdle nor a fence.

And the priest would join the laughter: "Oh," said he, "I put him in,
    For there's five and twenty sovereigns to be won.
And the poor would find it useful, if the chestnut chanced to win,
    And he'll maybe win when all is said and done!"
He had called him Faugh-a-ballagh, which is French for "clear the course",
    And his colours were a vivid shade of green:
All the Dooleys and O'Donnells were on Father Riley's horse,
    While the Orangemen were backing Mandarin!

It was Hogan, the dog poisoner — aged man and very wise,
  Who was camping in the racecourse with his swag,
And who ventured the opinion, to the township's great surprise,
  That the race would go to Father Riley's nag.
"You can talk about your riders — and the horse has not been schooled,
  And the fences is terrific, and the rest!
When the field is fairly going, then ye'll see ye've all been fooled,
  And the chestnut horse will battle with the best.

"For there's some has got condition, and they think the race is sure,
  And the chestnut horse will fall beneath the weight,
But the hopes of all the helpless, and the prayers of all the poor,
  Will be running by his side to keep him straight.

And it's what's the need of schoolin' or of workin' on the track,
 Whin the saints are there to guide him round the course!
I've prayed him over every fence — I've prayed him out and back!
 And I'll bet my cash on Father Riley's horse!"

Oh, the steeple was a caution! They went tearin' round and round,
 And the fences rang and rattled where they struck.
There was some that cleared the water — there was more fell in and
 drowned,
 Some blamed the men and others blamed the luck!
But the whips were flying freely when the field came into view,
 For the finish down the long green stretch of course,
And in front of all the flyers — jumpin' like a kangaroo,
 Came the rank outsider — Father Riley's horse!

Oh, the shouting and the cheering as he rattled past the post!
 For he left the others standing, in the straight;
And the rider — well they reckoned it was Andy Regan's ghost,
 And it beat 'em how a ghost would draw the weight!
But he weighed in, nine stone seven, then he laughed and disappeared,
 Like a banshee (which is Spanish for an elf),
And old Hogan muttered sagely, "If it wasn't for the beard
 They'd be thinking it was Andy Regan's self!"

And the poor of Kiley's Crossing drank the health at Christmastide
 Of the chestnut and his rider dressed in green.
There was never such a rider, not since Andy Regan died,
 And they wondered who on earth he could have been.
But they settled it among 'em, for the story got about,
 'Mongst the bushmen and the people on the course,
That the Devil had been ordered to let Andy Regan out
 For the steeplechase on Father Riley's horse!

SAWREY

Last Week

Oh, the new chum went to the backblock run,
  But he should have gone there last week.
He tramped ten miles with a loaded gun,
But of turkey or duck he saw never a one,
For he should have been there last week,
  They said,
There were flocks of 'em there last week.

He wended his way to a waterfall,
And he should have gone there last week.
He carried a camera, legs and all,
But the day was hot, and the stream was small,
For he should have gone there last week,
  They said,
They drowned a man there last week.

He went for a drive, and he made a start,
Which should have been made last week,
For the old horse died of a broken heart;
So he footed it home and he dragged the cart —
But the horse was all right last week,
  They said,
He trotted a match last week.

So he asked the bushies who came from far
To visit the town last week,
If they'd dine with him, and they said, "Hurrah!"
But there wasn't a drop in the whisky jar —
"You should have been here last week,"
  He said,
"I drank it all up last week!"

Waltzing Matilda

(Carrying a Swag)

Oh there once was a swagman camped in the billabongs,
  Under the shade of a Coolibah tree;
And he sang as he looked at the old billy boiling,
  "Who'll come a-waltzing Matilda with me."

Who'll come a-waltzing Matilda, my darling,
  Who'll come a-waltzing Matilda with me.
Waltzing Matilda and leading a water-bag,
  Who'll come a-waltzing Matilda with me.

Up came the jumbuck to drink at the waterhole,
  Up jumped the swagman and grabbed him in glee;
And he sang as he put him away in his tucker-bag,
  "You'll come a-waltzing Matilda with me."

Who'll come a-waltzing Matilda, my darling,
  Who'll come a-waltzing Matilda with me.
Waltzing Matilda and leading a water-bag,
  Who'll come a-waltzing Matilda with me.

Up came the squatter a-riding his thoroughbred;
  Up came policemen — one, two, and three.
"Whose is the jumbuck you've got in the tucker-bag?
  You'll come a-waltzing Matilda with we."

Who'll come a-waltzing Matilda, my darling,
  Who'll come a-waltzing Matilda with me.
Waltzing Matilda and leading a water-bag,
  Who'll come a-waltzing Matilda with me.

Up sprang the swagman and jumped in the waterhole,
  Drowning himself by the Coolibah tree;
And his voice can be heard as it sings in the billabongs,
  "Who'll come a-waltzing Matilda with me."

Who'll come a-waltzing Matilda, my darling,
  Who'll come a-waltzing Matilda with me.
Waltzing Matilda and leading a water-bag,
  Who'll come a-waltzing Matilda with me.

Old Pardon, the Son of Reprieve

You never heard tell of the story?
  Well, now, I can hardly believe!
Never heard of the honour and glory
  Of Pardon, the son of Reprieve?
But maybe you're only a Johnnie
  And don't know a horse from a hoe?
Well, well, don't get angry, my sonny,
  But, really, a young 'un should know.

They bred him out back on the "Never",
  His mother was Mameluke breed.
To the front — and then stay there — was ever
  The root of the Mameluke creed.
He seemed to inherit their wiry
  Strong frames — and their pluck to receive —
As hard as a flint and as fiery
  Was Pardon, the son of Reprieve.

We ran him at many a meeting
  At crossing and gully and town,
And nothing could give him a beating —
  At least when our money was down.
For weight wouldn't stop him, nor distance,
  Nor odds, though the others were fast,
He'd race with a dogged persistence,
  And wear them all down at the last.

At the Turon the Yattendon filly
  Led by lengths at the mile and a half,
And we all began to look silly,
  While *her* crowd were starting to laugh;

But the old horse came faster and faster,
    His pluck told its tale, and his strength,
He gained on her, caught her, and passed her,
    And won it, hands down, by a length.

And then we swooped down on Menindie
    To run for the President's Cup —
Oh! that's a sweet township — a shindy
    To them is board, lodging, and sup.
Eye-openers they are, and their system
    Is never to suffer defeat;
It's "win, tie, or wrangle" — to best 'em
    You must lose 'em, or else it's "dead heat".

We strolled down the township and found 'em
    At drinking and gaming and play;
If sorrows they had, why they drowned 'em,
    And betting was soon under way.
Their horses were good 'uns and fit 'uns,
    There was plenty of cash in the town;
They backed their own horses like Britons,
    And Lord! how *we* rattled it down!

With gladness we thought of the morrow,
    We counted our wagers with glee,
A simile homely to borrow —
    "There was plenty of milk in our tea".
You see we were green; and we never
    Had even a thought of foul play,
Though we well might have known that the clever
    Division would "put us away".

Experience "*docet*", they tell us,
    At least so I've frequently heard,
But, "dosing" or "stuffing", those fellows
    Were up to each move on the board;

They got to his stall — it is sinful
    To think what such villains would do —
And they gave him a regular skinful
    Of barley — green barley — to chew.

He munched it all night, and we found him
    Next morning as full as a hog —
The girths wouldn't nearly meet round him;
    He looked like an overfed frog.
We saw we were done like a dinner —
    The odds were a thousand to one
Against Pardon turning up winner,
    'Twas cruel to ask him to run.

We got to the course with our troubles,
    A crestfallen couple were we;
And we heard the "books" calling the doubles —
    A roar like the surf of the sea;
And over the tumult and louder
    Rang, "Any price Pardon, I lay!"
Says Jimmy, "The children of Judah
    Are out on the warpath to-day."

Three miles in three heats: Ah, my sonny
    The horses in those days were stout,
They had to run well to win money;
    I don't see such horses about.
Your six-furlong vermin that scamper
    Half a mile with their featherweight up;
They wouldn't earn much of their damper
    In a race like the President's Cup.

The first heat was soon set a-going;
    The Dancer went off to the front;
The Don on his quarters was showing,
    With Pardon right out of the hunt.

68

He rolled and he weltered and wallowed —
    You'd kick your hat faster, I'll bet;
They finished all bunched, and he followed
    All lathered and dripping with sweat.

But troubles came thicker upon us,
    For while we were rubbing him dry
The stewards came over to warn us:
    "We hear you are running a bye!
If Pardon don't spiel like tarnation
    And win the next heat — if he can —
He'll earn a disqualification;
    Just think over *that*, now, my man!"

Our money all gone and our credit,
    Our horse couldn't gallop a yard;
And then people thought that *we* did it!
    It really was terribly hard.

We were objects of mirth and derision
    To folk in the lawn and the stand,
And the yells of the clever division
    Of "Any price, Pardon!" were grand.

We still had a chance for the money,
    Two heats still remained to be run;
If both fell to us — why, my sonny,
    The clever division were done.
And Pardon was better, we reckoned,
    His sickness was passing away,
So he went to the post for the second
    And principal heat of the day.

They're off and away with a rattle,
    Like dogs from the leashes let slip,
And right at the back of the battle
    He followed them under the whip.

They gained ten good lengths on him quickly,
    He dropped right away from the pack;
I tell you it made me feel sickly
    To see the blue jacket fall back.

Our very last hope had departed —
    We thought the old fellow was done,
When all of a sudden he started
    To go like a shot from a gun.
His chances seemed slight to embolden
    Our hearts; but, with teeth firmly set,
We thought, "Now or never! The old 'un
    May reckon with some of 'em yet."

Then loud rose the war-cry for Pardon;
    He swept like the wind down the dip,
And over the rise by the garden,
    The jockey was done with the whip;
The field were at sixes and sevens —
    The pace at the first had been fast —
And hope seemed to drop from the heavens,
    For Pardon was coming at last.

And how he did come! It was splendid;
    He gained on them yards every bound,
Stretching out like a greyhound extended,
    His girth laid right down on the ground.
A shimmer of silk in the cedars
    As into the running they wheeled,
And out flashed the whips on the leaders,
    For Pardon had collared the field.

Then right through the ruck he came sailing —
    I knew that the battle was won —
The son of Haphazard was failing,
    The Yattendon filly was done;

He cut down the Don and the Dancer,
    He raced clean away from the mare —
He's in front! Catch him now if you can, sir!
    And up went my hat in the air!

Then loud from the lawn and the garden
    Rose offers of "Ten to one *on*!"
"Who'll bet on the field? I back Pardon!"
    No use; all the money was gone.
He came for the third heat light-hearted,
    A-jumping and dancing about;
The others were done ere they started
    Crestfallen, and tired, and worn out.

He won it, and ran it much faster
    Than even the first, I believe
Oh, he was the daddy, the master,
    Was Pardon, the son of Reprieve.
He showed 'em the method to travel —
    The boy sat as still as a stone —
They never could see him for gravel;
    He came in hard-held, and alone.

But he's old — and his eyes are grown hollow;
    Like me, with my thatch of the snow;
When he dies, then I hope I may follow,
    And go where the racehorses go.
I don't want no harping nor singing —
    Such things with my style don't agree;
Where the hoofs of the horses are ringing
    There's music sufficient for me.

And surely the thoroughbred horses
    Will rise up again and begin
Fresh races on faraway courses

74

And p'raps they might let me slip in.
It would look rather well the race card on
    'Mongst cherubs and seraphs and things,
"Angel Harrison's black gelding Pardon,
    Blue halo, white body and wings".

And if they have racing hereafter,
    (And who is to say they will not?)
When the cheers and the shouting and laughter
    Proclaim that the battle grows hot;
As they come down the racecourse a-steering,
    He'll rush to the front, I believe;
And you'll hear the great multitude cheering
    For Pardon, the son of Reprieve.

Mulga Bill's Bicycle

'Twas Mulga Bill, from Eaglehawk, that caught the cycling craze;
He turned away the good old horse that served him many days;
He dressed himself in cycling clothes, resplendent to be seen;
He hurried off to town and bought a shining new machine;
And as he wheeled it through the door, with air of lordly pride,
The grinning shop assistant said, "Excuse me, can you ride?"

"See here, young man," said Mulga Bill, "from Walgett to the sea,
From Conroy's Gap to Castlereagh, there's none can ride like me.
I'm good all round at everything, as everybody knows,
Although I'm not the one to talk — I *hate* a man that blows.
But riding is my special gift, my chiefest, sole delight;
Just ask a wild duck can it swim, a wildcat can it fight.
There's nothing clothed in hair or hide, or built of flesh or steel,
There's nothing walks or jumps, or runs, on axle, hoof, or wheel,
But what I'll sit, while hide will hold and girths and straps are tight:
I'll ride this here two-wheeled concern right straight away at sight."

'Twas Mulga Bill, from Eaglehawk, that sought his own abode,
That perched above the Dead Man's Creek, beside the mountain road.
He turned the cycle down the hill and mounted for the fray,
But ere he'd gone a dozen yards it bolted clean away.
It left the track, and through the trees, just like a silver streak,
It whistled down the awful slope towards the Dead Man's Creek.

It shaved a stump by half an inch, it dodged a big white-box:
The very wallaroos in fright went scrambling up the rocks,
The wombats hiding in their caves dug deeper underground,
As Mulga Bill, as white as chalk, sat tight to every bound.
It struck a stone and gave a spring that cleared a fallen tree,
It raced beside a precipice as close as close could be;

And then as Mulga Bill let out one last despairing shriek
It made a leap of twenty feet into the Dead Man's Creek.

'Twas Mulga Bill, from Eaglehawk, that slowly swam ashore:
He said, "I've had some narrer shaves and lively rides before;
I've rode a wild bull round a yard to win a five-pound bet,
But this was the most awful ride that I've encountered yet.
I'll give that two-wheeled outlaw best; it's shaken all my nerve
To feel it whistle through the air and plunge and buck and swerve.
It's safe at rest in Dead Man's Creek, we'll leave it lying still;
A horse's back is good enough henceforth for Mulga Bill."

The Geebung Polo Club

It was somewhere up the country, in a land of rock and scrub,
That they formed an institution called the Geebung Polo Club.
They were long and wiry natives from the rugged mountainside,
And the horse was never saddled that the Geebungs couldn't ride;
But their style of playing polo was irregular and rash —
They had mighty little science, but a mighty lot of dash:
And they played on mountain ponies that were muscular and strong,
Though their coats were quite unpolished, and their manes and tails were long.
And they used to train those ponies wheeling cattle in the scrub:
They were demons, were the members of the Geebung Polo Club.

It was somewhere down the country, in a city's smoke and steam,
That a polo club existed, called the Cuff and Collar Team.
As a social institution 'twas a marvellous success,
For the members were distinguished by exclusiveness and dress.
They had natty little ponies that were nice, and smooth, and sleek,
For their cultivated owners only rode 'em once a week.
So they started up the country in pursuit of sport and fame,
For they meant to show the Geebungs how they ought to play the game;
And they took their valets with them — just to give their boots a rub
Ere they started operations on the Geebung Polo Club.

Now my readers can imagine how the contest ebbed and flowed,
When the Geebung boys got going it was time to clear the road;
And the game was so terrific that ere half the time was gone
A spectator's leg was broken — just from merely looking on.
For they waddied one another till the plain was strewn with dead,
While the score was kept so even that they neither got ahead.
And the Cuff and Collar captain, when he tumbled off to die,
Was the last surviving player — so the game was called a tie.

Then the captain of the Geebungs raised him slowly from the ground,
Though his wounds were mostly mortal, yet he fiercely gazed around;
There was no one to oppose him — all the rest were in a trance,
So he scrambled on his pony for his last expiring chance,
For he meant to make an effort to get victory to his side;
So he struck at goal — and missed it — then he tumbled off and died.

By the old Campaspe River, where the breezes shake the grass,
There's a row of little gravestones that the stockmen never pass,
For they bear a crude inscription saying, "Stranger, drop a tear,
For the Cuff and Collar players and the Geebung boys lie here."
And on misty moonlit evenings, while the dingoes howl around,
You can see their shadows flitting down that phantom polo ground;
You can hear the loud collisions as the flying players meet,
And the rattle of the mallets, and the rush of ponies' feet,
Till the terrified spectator rides like blazes to the pub —
He's been haunted by the spectres of the Geebung Polo Club.

Those Names

The shearers sat in the firelight, hearty and hale and strong,
After the hard day's shearing, passing the joke along:
The "ringer" that shore a hundred, as they never were shorn before,
And the novice who, toiling bravely, had tommyhawked half a score,
The tar boy, the cook, and the slushy, the sweeper that swept the board,
The picker-up, and the penner, with the rest of the shearing horde.
There were men from the inland stations where the skies like a furnace glow,
And men from the Snowy River, the land of the frozen snow;
There were swarthy Queensland drovers who reckoned all land by miles,
And farmers' sons from the Murray, where many a vineyard smiles.
They started at telling stories when they wearied of cards and games,
And to give these stories a flavour they threw in some local names,
And a man from the bleak Monaro, away on the tableland,
He fixed his eyes on the ceiling, and he started to play his hand.

He told them of Adjintoothbong, where the pine-clad mountains freeze,
And the weight of the snow in summer breaks branches off the trees,
And, as he warmed to the business, he let them have it strong —
Nimitybelle, Conargo, Wheeo, Bongongolong;
He lingered over them fondly, because they recalled to mind
A thought of the old bush homestead, and the girl that he left behind.
Then the shearers all sat silent till a man in the corner rose;
Said he, "I've travelled aplenty but never heard names like those,
Out in the western districts, out on the Castlereagh
Most of the names are easy — short for a man to say.
"You've heard of Mungrybambone and the Gundabluey pine,
Quobbotha, Girilambone, and Terramungamine,
Quambone, Eunonyhareenha, Wee Waa, and Buntijo —"

But the rest of the shearers stopped him, "For the sake of your jaw, go slow,
If you reckon those names are short ones out where such names prevail,
Just try and remember some long ones before you begin the tale."

And the man from the western district, though never a word he said,
Just winked with his dexter eyelid, and then he retired to bed.

Driver Smith

'Twas Driver Smith of Battery A was anxious to see a fight;
    He thought of the Transvaal all the day, he thought of it all the
    night —
"Well, if the battery's left behind, I'll go to the war," says he,
"I'll go a-driving an ambulance in the ranks of the A.M.C.

"I'm fairly sick of these here parades, it's want of a change that kills
A-charging the Randwick Rifle Range and aiming at Surry Hills.
And I think if I go with the ambulance I'm certain to find a show,
For they have to send the medical men wherever the troops can go.

"Wherever the rifle bullets flash and the Maxims raise a din,
It's there you'll find the medical men a-raking the wounded in —
A-raking 'em in like human flies — and a driver smart like me
Will find some scope for his extra skill in the ranks of the A.M.C."

So Driver Smith he went to the war a-cracking his driver's whip,
From ambulance to collecting base they showed him his regular trip.
And he said to the boys that were marching past, as he gave his whip a
    crack,
"You'll walk yourselves to the fight," says he — "Lord spare me, I'll drive
    you back."

Now, the fight went on in the Transvaal hills for the half of a day or more,
And Driver Smith he worked his trip — all aboard for the seat of war!
He took his load from the stretcher men and hurried 'em homeward fast
Till he heard a sound he knew full well — a battery rolling past.

He heard the clink of the leading chains and the roll of the guns
    behind —
He heard the crack of the drivers' whips, and he says to 'em, "Strike me
    blind,

I'll miss me trip with this ambulance, although I don't care to shirk,
But I'll take the car off the line to-day and follow the guns at work."

Then up the Battery Colonel came a-cursing 'em black in the face.
"Sit down and shift 'em, you drivers there, and gallop 'em into place."
So off the Battery rolled and swung, a-going a merry dance,
And holding his own with the leading gun goes Smith with his ambulance.

They opened fire on the mountainside, a-peppering by and large,
When over the hill above their flank the Boers came down at the charge;
They rushed the guns with a daring rush, a-volleying left and right,
And Driver Smith with his ambulance moved up to the edge of the fight.

The gunners stuck to their guns like men, and fought like the wild cats fight,
For a Battery man don't leave his gun with ever a hope in sight;
But the bullets sang and the Mausers cracked and the Battery men gave
     way,
Till Driver Smith with his ambulance drove into the thick of the fray.

He saw the head of the Transvaal troop a-thundering to and fro,
A hard old face with a monkey beard — a face that he seemed to know;
"Now, who's that leader," said Driver Smith, "I've seen him before to-day.
Why, bless my heart, but it's Kruger's self", and he jumped for him
     straight away.

He collared old Kruger round the waist and hustled him into the van.
It wasn't according to stretcher drill for raising a wounded man;
But he forced him in and said: "All aboard, we're off for a little ride,
And you'll have the car to yourself," says he, "I reckon we're full inside."

He wheeled his team on the mountainside and set 'em a merry pace,
A-galloping over the rocks and stones, and a lot of the Boers gave chase;
But Driver Smith had a fairish start, and he said to the Boers, "Good-day,
You have Buckley's chance for to catch a man that was trained in
     Battery A."

He drove his team to the hospital and said to the P.M.O.,
"Beg pardon, sir, but I missed a trip, mistaking the way to go;
And Kruger came to the ambulance and asked could we spare a bed,
So I fetched him here, and we'll take him home to show for a bob a head."

So the word went round to the English troops to say they need fight
    no more,
For Driver Smith with his ambulance had ended the blooming war:
And in London now at the music halls he's starring it every night,
And drawing a hundred pounds a week to tell how he won the fight.

Saltbush Bill's Second Fight

The news came down on the Castlereagh, and went to the world at large,
  That twenty thousand travelling sheep, with Saltbush Bill in charge,
Were drifting down from a dried-out run to ravage the Castlereagh;
And the squatters swore when they heard the news, and wished they
    were well away:
For the name and the fame of Saltbush Bill were over the countryside
For the wonderful way that he fed his sheep, and the dodges and tricks
    he tried.
He would lose his way on a Main Stock Route, and stray to the
    squatters' grass;
He would come to a run with the boss away, and swear he had leave
    to pass;
And back of all and behind it all, as well the squatters knew,
If he had to fight, he would fight all day, so long as his sheep got through:
But this is the story of Stingy Smith, the owner of Hard Times Hill,
And the way that he chanced on a fighting man to reckon with
    Saltbush Bill.

'Twas Stingy Smith on his stockyard sat, and prayed for an early spring,
When he started at sight of a clean-shaved tramp, who walked with
    jaunty swing;
For a clean-shaved tramp with a jaunty walk a-swinging along the track
Is as rare a thing as a feathered frog on the desolate roads outback.
So the tramp he made for the travellers' hut, and asked could he camp
    the night;
But Stingy Smith had a bright idea, and he said to him, "Can you fight?"
"Why, what's the game?" said the clean-shaved tramp, as he looked at him
    up and down —
"If you want a battle, get off that fence, and I'll kill you for half-a-crown!
But, Boss, you'd better not fight with me, it wouldn't be fair nor right;
I'm Stiffener Joe, from the Rocks Brigade, and I killed a man in a fight:

I served two years for it, fair and square, and now I'm a-trampin' back,
To look for a peaceful quiet life away on the outside track —"
"Oh, it's not myself, but a drover chap," said Stingy Smith with glee;
"A bullying fellow, called Saltbush Bill — and you are the man for me.
He's on the road with his hungry sheep, and he's certain to raise a row,
For he's bullied the whole of the Castlereagh till he's got them
      under cow —
Just pick a quarrel and raise a fight, and leather him good and hard,
And I'll take good care that his wretched sheep don't wander a half a yard.
It's a five-pound job if you belt him well — do anything short of kill,
For there isn't a beak on the Castlereagh will fine you for Saltbush Bill."

"I'll take the job," said the fighting man, "and hot as this cove appears,
He'll stand no chance with a bloke like me, what's lived on the game
      for years;
For he's maybe learnt in a boxing school, and sparred for a round or so,
But I've fought all hands in a ten foot ring each night in a travelling show;
They earnt a pound if they stayed three rounds, and they tried for it
      every night —
In a ten foot ring! Oh, that's the game that teaches a bloke to fight,
For they'd rush and clinch, it was Dublin Rules, and we drew no colour
      line;
And they all tried hard for to earn the pound, but they got no pound
      of mine:
If I saw no chance in the opening round I'd slog at their wind, and wait
Till an opening came — and it *always* came — and I settled 'em, sure
      as fate;
Left on the ribs and right on the jaw — and, when the chance comes,
      make sure!
And it's there a professional bloke like me gets home on an amateur:

"For it's my experience every day, and I make no doubt it's yours,
That a third-class pro is an over-match for the best of the amateurs —"
"Oh, take your swag to the travellers' hut," said Smith, "for you waste
      your breath;

You've a first-class chance, if you lose the fight, of talking your man
      to death.
I'll tell the cook you're to have your grub, and see that you eat your fill,
And come to the scratch all fit and well to leather this Saltbush Bill.''

'Twas Saltbush Bill, and his travelling sheep were wending their
      weary way
On the Main Stock Route, through the Hard Times Run, on their six-mile
      stage a day;
And he strayed a mile from the Main Stock Route, and started to
      feed along,
And, when Stingy Smith came up, Bill said that the Route was
      surveyed wrong;
And he tried to prove that the sheep had rushed and strayed from their
      camp at night,
But the fighting man he kicked Bill's dog, and of course that meant a fight:

So they sparred and fought, and they shifted ground and never a sound
    was heard
But the thudding fists on their brawny ribs, and the seconds' muttered
    word,
Till the fighting man shot home his left on the ribs with a mighty clout,
And his right flashed up with a half-arm blow — and Saltbush Bill
    "went out".
He fell face down, and towards the blow; and their hearts with fear
    were filled,
For he lay as still as a fallen tree, and they thought that he must be killed.

So Stingy Smith and the fighting man, they lifted him from the ground,
And sent to home for a brandy flask, and they slowly fetched him
    round;
But his head was bad, and his jaw was hurt — in fact, he could scarcely
    speak —
So they let him spell till he got his wits, and he camped on the run a week,

While the travelling sheep went here and there, wherever they liked
    to stray,
Till Saltbush Bill was fit once more for the track to the Castlereagh.

Then Stingy Smith he wrote a note, and gave to the fighting man:
'Twas writ to the boss of the neighbouring run, and thus the missive ran:
"The man with this is a fighting man, one Stiffener Joe by name;
He came near murdering Saltbush Bill, and I found it a costly game:
But it's worth your while to employ the chap, for there isn't the
    slightest doubt
You'll have no trouble from Saltbush Bill while this man hangs about —"
But an answer came by the next week's mail, with news that might
    well appal:
"The man you sent with a note is not a fighting man at all!
He has shaved his beard, and has cut his hair, but I spotted him at a look;
He is Tom Devine, who has worked for years for Saltbush Bill as cook.
Bill coached him up in the fighting yarn, and taught him the tale by rote,
And they shammed to fight, and they got your grass and divided your
    five-pound note.
'Twas a clean take-in, and you'll find it wise — 'twill save you a lot
    of pelf —
When next you're hiring a fighting man, just fight him a round yourself."

And the teamsters out on the Castlereagh, when they meet with a week
    of rain,
And the waggon sinks to its axle-tree, deep down in the black soil plain,
When the bullocks wade in a sea of mud, and strain at the load of wool,
And the cattle dogs at the bullocks' heels are biting to make them pull,
When the offside driver flays the team, and curses them while he flogs,
And the air is thick with the language used, and the clamour of men
    and dogs —
The teamsters say, as they pause to rest and moisten each hairy throat,
They wish they could swear like Stingy Smith when he read that
    neighbour's note.

94

The Travelling Post Office

The roving breezes come and go, the reed beds sweep and sway,
  The sleepy river murmurs low, and loiters on its way,
It is the land of lots o' time along the Castlereagh.

The old man's son had left the farm, he found it dull and slow,
He drifted to the great north-west where all the rovers go.
"He's gone so long," the old man said, "he's dropped right out of mind,
But if you'd write a line to him I'd take it very kind;
He's shearing here and fencing there, a kind of waif and stray,
He's droving now with Conroy's sheep along the Castlereagh.
The sheep are travelling for the grass, and travelling very slow;
They may be at Mundooran now, or past the Overflow,
Or tramping down the black soil flats across by Waddiwong,
But all those little country towns would send the letter wrong,
The mailman, if he's extra tired, would pass them in his sleep,
It's safest to address the note to 'Care of Conroy's sheep',
For five and twenty thousand head can scarcely go astray,
You write to 'Care of Conroy's sheep along the Castlereagh'."

By rock and ridge and riverside the western mail has gone,
Across the great Blue Mountain Range to take that letter on.
A moment on the topmost grade while open fire doors glare,
She pauses like a living thing to breathe the mountain air,
Then launches down the other side across the plains away
To bear that note to "Conroy's sheep along the Castlereagh".

And now by coach and mailman's bag it goes from town to town,
And Conroy's Gap and Conroy's Creek have marked it "further down".
Beneath a sky of deepest blue where never cloud abides,
A speck upon the waste of plain the lonely mailman rides.
Where fierce hot winds have set the pine and myall boughs asweep
He hails the shearers passing by for news of Conroy's sheep.

95

By big lagoons where wildfowl play and crested pigeons flock,
By campfires where the drovers ride around their restless stock,
And past the teamster toiling down to fetch the wool away
My letter chases Conroy's sheep along the Castlereagh.

An Evening in Dandaloo

It was while we held our races —
Hurdles, sprints and steeplechases —
    Up in Dandaloo,
That a crowd of Sydney stealers,
Jockeys, pugilists and spielers
Brought some horses, real heelers,
    Came and put us through.

Beat our nags and won our money,
Made the game by no means funny,
    Made us rather blue;
When the racing was concluded,
Of our hard-earned coin denuded
Dandaloonies sat and brooded
    There in Dandaloo.

Night came down on Johnson's shanty
Where the grog was no means scanty,
    And a tumult grew
Till some wild, excited person
Galloped down the township cursing,
"Sydney push have mobbed Macpherson,
    Roll up, Dandaloo!"

Great St Denis! what commotion!
Like the rush of stormy ocean
    Fiery horsemen flew.
Dust and smoke and din and rattle,
Down the street they spurred their cattle
To the war-cry of the battle,
    "Wade in, Dandaloo!"

So the boys might have their fight out,
Johnson blew the bar-room light out,
     Then in haste, withdrew.
And in darkness and in doubting
Raged the conflict and the shouting,
"Give the Sydney push a clouting,
     Go it, Dandaloo!"

Jack Macpherson seized a bucket,
Every head he saw, he struck it —
     Struck in earnest, too;
And a man from Lower Wattle,
Whom a shearer tried to throttle,
Hit out freely with a bottle,
   ` There in Dandaloo.

Skin and hair were flying thickly,
When a light was fetched, and quickly
     Brought a fact to view —
On the scene of the diversion
Every single, solid person
Came along to help Macpherson —
     All were Dandaloo!

When the list of slain was tabled,
Some were drunk and some disabled,
     Still, we found it true.
In the darkness and the smother
We'd been belting one another;
Jack Macpherson bashed his brother
     There in Dandaloo.

So we drank, and all departed —
How the "mobbing" yarn was started
     No one ever knew —

And the stockmen tell the story
Of that conflict fierce and gory,
How we fought for love and glory
   Up in Dandaloo.

It's a proverb now, or near it —
At the races you can hear it,
   At the dog fights, too;
Every shrieking, dancing drover,
As the canines topple over,
Yells applause to Grip or Rover,
   "Give him 'Dandaloo'!"

And the teamster slowly toiling
Through the deep black country soiling
   Wheels and axles, too,
Lays the whip on Spot and Banker,
Rouses Tarboy with a flanker —
"Redman! Ginger! Heave there! Yank her!
   Wade in, Dandaloo!"

A Grain of Desert Sand

Beneath the blue Egyptian skies,
  With ramp and roller, guide and stay,
I saw the Pyramids arise
    And I shall see them pass away.

I watched when Alexander passed;
    I saw Napoleon's flag unfurled —
The greatest and perhaps the last
    Of men whose footsteps shook the world.

To each his hour of pride and place,
    Arab and Persian, Greek and Jew;
Mahomet trod upon my face,
    Darius spurned me with his shoe.

And yet I am not Priest or King,
    Sultan or Chief in high command.
I am that one unchanging thing,
    A grain of desert sand.

By the Grey Gulf-water

F ar to the northward there lies a land,
  A wonderful land that the winds blow over,
And none may fathom nor understand
  The charm it holds for the restless rover;
A great grey chaos — a land half made,
  Where endless space is and no life stirreth;
And the soul of a man will recoil afraid
  From the sphinx-like visage that Nature weareth.
But old Dame Nature, though scornful, craves
  Her dole of death and her share of slaughter;
Many indeed are the nameless graves
  Where her victims sleep by the Grey Gulf-water.

Slowly and slowly those grey streams glide,
  Drifting along with a languid motion,
Lapping the reed beds on either side,
  Wending their way to the Northern Ocean.
Grey are the plains where the emus pass
  Silent and slow, with their staid demeanour;
Over the dead men's graves the grass
  Maybe is waving a trifle greener.
Down in the world where men toil and spin
  Dame Nature smiles as man's hand has taught her;
Only the dead men her smiles can win
  In the great lone land by the Grey Gulf-water.

For the strength of man is an insect's strength,
  In the face of that mighty plain and river,
And the life of a man is a moment's length
  To the life of the stream that will run for ever.
And so it cometh they take no part
  In small-world worries; each hardy rover

Rideth abroad and is light of heart,
   With the plains around and the blue sky over.
And up in the heavens the brown lark sings
   The songs that the strange wild land has taught her;
Full of thanksgiving her sweet song rings —
   And I wish I were back by the Grey Gulf-water.

A Bush Christening

O n the outer Barcoo where the churches are few,
  And men of religion are scanty,
On a road never cross'd 'cept by folk that are lost,
  One Michael Magee had a shanty.

Now this Mike was the dad of a ten-year-old lad,
  Plump, healthy, and stoutly conditioned;
He was strong as the best, but poor Mike had no rest
  For the youngster had never been christened.

And his wife used to cry, "If the darlin' should die
  Saint Peter would not recognise him."
But by luck he survived till a preacher arrived,
  Who agreed straightaway to baptise him.

Now the artful young rogue, while they held their collogue,
  With his ear to the keyhole was listenin',
And he muttered in fright while his features turned white,
  "What the divil and all is this christenin'?"

He was none of your dolts, he had seen them brand colts,
  And it seemed to his small understanding,
If the man in the frock made him one of the flock,
  It must mean something very like branding.

So away with a rush he set off for the bush,
  While the tears in his eyelids they glistened —
"'Tis outrageous," says he, "to brand youngsters like me,
  I'll be dashed if I'll stop to be christened!"

Like a young native dog he ran into a log,
  And his father with language uncivil,

Never heeding the "praste" cried aloud in his haste,
"Come out and be christened, you divil!"

But he lay there as snug as a bug in a rug,
And his parents in vain might reprove him,
Till his reverence spoke (he was fond of a joke)
"I've a notion," says he, "that'll move him.

"Poke a stick up the log, give the spalpeen a prog;
Poke him aisy — don't hurt him or maim him,
'Tis not long that he'll stand, I've the water at hand,
As he rushes out this end I'll name him.

"Here he comes, and for shame! ye've forgotten the name —
Is it Patsy or Michael or Dinnis?"
Here the youngster ran out, and the priest gave a shout —
"Take your chance, anyhow, wid 'Maginnis'!"

As the howling young cub ran away to the scrub
Where he knew that pursuit would be risky,
The priest, as he fled, flung a flask at his head
That was labelled "Maginnis's Whisky!"

And Maginnis Magee has been made a J.P.,
And the one thing he hates more than sin is
To be asked by the folk who have heard of the joke,
How he came to be christened "Maginnis"!

The Uplift

When the drays are bogged and sinking, then it's no use sitting thinking,
  You must put the teams together and must double-bank the pull.
When the crop is light and weedy, or the fleece is burred and seedy,
  Then the next year's crop and fleeces may repay you to the full.

  So it's lift her, Johnny, lift her,
  Put your back in it and shift her,
While the jabber, jabber, jabber of the politicians flows.
  If your nag's too poor to travel
  Then get down and scratch the gravel
For you'll get there if you walk it — if you don't, you'll feed the crows.

Shall we waste our time debating with a grand young country waiting
  For the plough and for the harrow and the lucerne and the maize?
For it's work alone will save us in the land that fortune gave us
  There's no crop but what we'll grow it; there's no stock but what we'll raise.

  When the team is bogged and sinking
  Then it's no use sitting thinking.
There's a roadway up the mountain that the old black leader knows:
  So it's lift her, Johnny, lift her,
  Put your back in it and shift her,
Take a lesson from the bullock — he goes slowly, but he goes!

The Amateur Rider

Him going to ride for us! *Him* — with the pants and the eyeglass and all.
Amateur! don't he just look it — it's twenty to one on a fall.
Boss must be gone off his head to be sending our steeplechase crack
Out over fences like these with an object like that on his back.

Ride! Don't tell *me* he can ride. With his pants just as loose as balloons,
How can he sit on his horse? And his spurs like a pair of harpoons;
Ought to be under the Dog Act, he ought, and be kept off the course.
Fall! why, he'd fall off a cart, let alone off a steeplechase horse.

Yessir! the 'orse is all ready — I wish you'd have rode him before;
Nothing like knowing your 'orse, sir, and this chap's a terror to bore;
Battleaxe always could pull, and he rushes his fences like fun —
Stands off his jump twenty feet, and then springs like a shot from a gun.

Oh, he can jump 'em all right, sir, you make no mistake, 'e's a toff;
Clouts 'em in earnest, too, sometimes, you mind that he don't clout
    you off —
Don't seem to mind how he hits 'em, his shins is as hard as a nail,
Sometimes you'll see the fence shake and the splinters fly up from the rail.

All you can do is to hold him and just let him jump as he likes,
Give him his head at the fences, and hang on like death if he strikes;
Don't let him run himself out — you can lie third or fourth in the race —
Until you clear the stone wall, and from that you can put on the pace.

Fell at that wall once, he did, and it gave him a regular spread,
Ever since that time he flies it — he'll stop if you pull at his head,
Just let him race — you can trust him — he'll take first-class care he
    don't fall,
And I think that's the lot — but remember, *he must have his head at
    the wall.*

Well, he's down safe as far as the start, and he seems to sit on pretty neat,
Only his baggified breeches would ruinate anyone's seat —
They're away — here they come — the first fence, and he's head over
    heels for a crown!
Good for the new chum, he's over, and two of the others are down!

Now for the treble, my hearty — By Jove, he can ride, after all;
Whoop, that's your sort — let him fly them! He hasn't much fear of a fall.
Who in the world would have thought it? And aren't they just going
    a pace?
Little Recruit in the lead there will make it a stoutly run race.

Lord! But they're racing in earnest — and down goes Recruit on his head,
Rolling clean over his boy — it's a miracle if he ain't dead.
Battleaxe, Battleaxe yet! By the Lord, he's got most of 'em beat —
Ho! did you see how he struck, and the swell never moved in his seat?

Second time round, and, by Jingo! he's holding his lead of 'em well;
Hark to him clouting the timber! It don't seem to trouble the swell.
Now for the wall — let him rush it. A thirty-foot leap, I declare —
Never a shift in his seat, and he's racing for home like a hare.

What's that that's chasing him — Rataplan — regular demon to stay!
Sit down and ride for your life now! Oh, good, that's the style —
    come away!
Rataplan's certain to beat you, unless you can give him the slip;
Sit down and rub in the whalebone now — give him the spurs and
    the whip!

Battleaxe, Battleaxe, yet — and it's Battleaxe wins for a crown;
Look at him rushing the fences, he wants to bring t'other chap down.
Rataplan never will catch him if only he keeps on his pins;
Now! the last fence! and he's over it! Battleaxe, Battleaxe wins!

Well, sir, you rode him just perfect — I knew from the first you could ride.
Some of the chaps said you couldn't, an' I says just like this a' one side:
Mark me, I says, that's a tradesman — the saddle is where he was bred.
Weight! you're all right, sir, and thank you; and them was the words that
      I said.

Shearing with a Hoe

The track that led to Carmody's is choked and overgrown,
The suckers of the stringybark have made the place their own;
The mountain rains have cut the track that once we used to know
When first we rode to Carmody's, a score of years ago.

The shearing shed at Carmody's was slab and stringybark,
The press was just a lever beam, invented in the Ark;
But Mrs Carmody was cook — and shearers' hearts would glow
With praise of grub at Carmody's, a score of years ago.

At shearing time no penners-up would curse their fate and weep,
For Fragrant Fred — the billy-goat — was trained to lead the sheep;
And racing down the rattling chutes the bleating mob would go
Behind their horned man from Cook's, a score of years ago.

An owner of the olden time, his patriarchal shed
Was innocent of all machines or gadgets overhead:
And pieces, locks and super-fleece together used to go
To fill the bales at Carmody's, a score of years ago.

A ringer from the western sheds, whose fame was wide and deep,
Was asked to take a vacant pen and shear a thousand sheep.
"Of course we've only got the blades!" "Well, what I want to know:
Why don't you get a bloke to take it off 'em with a hoe?"

In the Stable

W hat! You don't like him; well, maybe — we all have our fancies,
    of course:
Brumby to look at you reckon? Well, no: he's a thoroughbred horse;
Sired by a son of old Panic — look at his ears and his head —
Lop-eared and Roman-nosed, ain't he? — well, that's how the Panics
    are bred.
Gluttonous, ugly and lazy, rough as a tip-cart to ride,
Yet if you offered a sovereign apiece for the hairs on his hide
That wouldn't buy him, nor twice that; while I've a pound to the good,
This here old stager stays by me and lives like a thoroughbred should:
Hunt him away from his bedding, and sit yourself down by the wall,
Till you hear how the old fellow saved me from Gilbert, O'Maley and Hall.

Gilbert and Hall and O'Maley, back in the bushranging days,
Made themselves kings of the district — ruled it in old-fashioned ways —
Robbing the coach and the escort, stealing our horses at night,
Calling sometimes at the homesteads and giving the women a fright:
Came to the station one morning — and why they did this no one
    knows —
Took a brood mare from the paddock — wanting some fun, I suppose —
Fastened a bucket beneath her, hung by a strap round her flank,
Then turned her loose in the timber back of the seven-mile tank.

Go! She went mad! She went tearing and screaming with fear through
    the trees,
While the curst bucket beneath her was banging her flanks and her knees.
Bucking and racing and screaming she ran to the back of the run,
Killed herself there in a gully; by God, but they paid for their fun!
Paid for it dear, for the black boys found tracks, and the bucket, and all,
And I swore that I'd live to get even with Gilbert, O'Maley and Hall.

117

Day after day then I chased them — 'course they had friends on the sly,
Friends who were willing to sell them to those who were willing to buy.
Early one morning we found them in camp at the Cockatoo Farm;
One of us shot at O'Maley and wounded him under the arm:
Ran them for miles in the ranges, till Hall, with his horse fairly beat,
Took to the rocks and we lost him — the others made good their retreat.
It was war to the knife then, I tell you, and once, on the door of my shed,
They nailed up a notice that offered a hundred reward for my head!
Then we heard they were gone from the district, they stuck up a coach
     in the west,
And I rode by myself in the paddocks, taking a bit of a rest,
Riding this colt as a youngster — awkward, half-broken and shy,
He wheeled round one day on a sudden; I looked, but I couldn't see why,
But I soon found out why, for before me, the hillside rose up like a wall,
And there on the top with their rifles were Gilbert, O'Maley and Hall!

'Twas a good three-mile run to the homestead — bad going, with plenty
of trees —
So I gathered the youngster together, and gripped at his ribs with my
knees.
'Twas a mighty poor chance to escape them! It puts a man's nerve to
the test
On a half-broken colt to be hunted by the best mounted men in the west.
But the half-broken colt was a racehorse! He lay down to work with a will,
Flashed through the scrub like a clean-skin — by Heavens we *flew* down
the hill!
Over a twenty-foot gully he swept with the spring of a deer
And they fired as we jumped, but they missed me — a bullet sang close
to my ear —
And the jump gained us ground, for they shirked it: but I saw as we raced
through the gap

That the rails at the homestead were fastened — I was caught like a rat
     in a trap.
Fenced with barbed wire was the paddock — barbed wire that would cut
     like a knife —
How was a youngster to clear it that never had jumped in his life?

Bang went a rifle behind me — the colt gave a spring, he was hit;
Straight at the sliprails I rode him — I felt him take hold of the bit;
Never a foot to the right or the left did he swerve in his stride,
Awkward and frightened, but honest, the sort it's a pleasure to ride!
Straight at the rails, where they'd fastened barbed wire on the top of
     the post,
Rose like a stag and went over, with hardly a scratch at the most;
Into the homestead I darted, and snatched down my gun from the wall,
And I tell you I made them step lively, Gilbert, O'Maley and Hall!

Yes! There's the mark of the bullet — he's got it inside of him yet
Mixed up somehow with his victuals, but bless you he don't seem to fret!
Gluttonous, ugly, and lazy — eats any thing he can bite;
Now, let us shut up the stable, and bid the old fellow goodnight:
Ah! We can't breed 'em, the sort that were bred when we old 'uns were
     young.
Yes, I was saying, these bushrangers, none of 'em lived to be hung,
Gilbert was shot by the troopers, Hall was betrayed by his friend,
Campbell disposed of O'Maley, bringing the lot to an end.

But you can talk about riding — I've ridden a lot in the past —
Wait till there's rifles behind you, you'll know what it means to go fast!
I've steeplechased, raced, and "run horses", but I think the most dashing
     of all
Was the ride when the old fellow saved me from Gilbert, O'Maley
     and Hall!

Black Swans

As I lie at rest on a patch of clover
In the western park when the day is done,
I watch as the wild black swans fly over
With their phalanx turned to the sinking sun;
And I hear the clang of their leader crying
To a lagging mate in the rearward flying,
And they fade away in the darkness dying,
Where the stars are mustering one by one.

Oh! ye wild black swans, 'twere a world of wonder
For a while to join in your westward flight,
With the stars above and the dim earth under,
Through the cooling air of the glorious night.
As we swept along on our pinions winging,
We should catch the chime of a church-bell ringing,
Or the distant note of a torrent singing,
Or the far-off flash of a station light.

From the northern lakes with the reeds and rushes,
Where the hills are clothed with a purple haze,
Where the bellbirds chime and the songs of thrushes
Make music sweet in the jungle maze,
They will hold their course to the westward ever,
Till they reach the banks of the old grey river,
Where the waters wash, and the reed beds quiver
In the burning heat of the summer days.

Oh! ye strange wild birds, will ye bear a greeting
To the folk that live in that western land?
Then for every sweep of your pinions beating,
Ye shall bear a wish to the sunburnt band,
To the stalwart men who are stoutly fighting

With the heat and drought and dust storm smiting,
Yet whose life somehow has a strange inviting,
When once to the work they have put their hand.

Facing it yet! Oh, my friend stout-hearted,
What does it matter for rain or shine,
For the hopes deferred and the gain departed?
Nothing could conquer that heart of thine.
And thy health and strength are beyond confessing
As the only joys that are worth possessing.
May the days to come be as rich in blessing
As the days we spent in the auld lang syne.

I would fain go back to the old grey river,
To the old bush days when our hearts were light,
But, alas! those days they have fled for ever,
They are like the swans that have swept from sight.
And I know full well that the strangers' faces
Would meet us now in our dearest places;
For our day is dead and has left no traces
But the thoughts that live in my mind tonight.

There are folk long dead, and our hearts would sicken —
We would grieve for them with a bitter pain,
If the past could live and the dead could quicken,
We then might turn to that life again.
But on lonely nights we would hear them calling,
We should hear their steps on the pathways falling,
We should loathe the life with a hate appalling
In our lonely rides by the ridge and plain.

In the silent park is a scent of clover,
And the distant roar of the town is dead,
And I hear once more as the swans fly over,
Their far-off clamour from overhead.

They are flying west by their instinct guided,
And for man likewise is his fate decided,
And griefs apportioned and joys divided
By a mighty power with a purpose dread.

Index of titles

Index of first lines of poems

Published in Australia in 2004 by
New Holland Publishers (Australia) Pty Ltd
Sydney • Auckland • London • Cape Town

14 Aquatic Drive Frenchs Forest NSW 2086 Australia
218 Lake Road Northcote Auckland New Zealand
86 Edgware Road London W2 2EA United Kingdom
80 McKenzie Street Cape Town 8001 South Africa

First published by Lansdowne in 1985
Reprinted by Weldon Publishing in 1989
Reprinted by Ure Smith Press in 1991, 1992
Reprinted by Lansdowne Publishing Pty Ltd 1995
Reprinted by New Holland Publishers 2004

National Library of Australia Cataloguing-in-Publication Data:

Paterson, A. B. (Andrew Barton), 1864-1941.
    The Banjo's best-loved poems.

    Includes index.
    ISBN 1 74110 241 3.

    I. Sawrey, Hugh, 1923- . II. Title.

A821.2

Publisher: Louise Egerton
Designer: Pam Prewster
Typesetter: Savage Type, Brisbane
Printer: Kyodo Printing, Singapore